IMAGES
of America

DUTCH ISLAND
AND FORT GREBLE

From 1898 to well into the 1920s, Fort Greble was the site of much activity, with troops coming and going at all times. Capable of housing and sustaining a permanent cadre of 327 Coast Artillery Corps personnel in permanent barracks, the island facility could also accommodate transient militia and national guard units for short term training periods as needs arose. This photograph, taken in 1915, shows a group of men arriving. (Jamestown Historical Society.)

IMAGES
of America

DUTCH ISLAND
AND FORT GREBLE

Walter K. Schroder

ARCADIA

First published 1998
Copyright © Walter K. Schroder, 1998

ISBN 0-7524-0897-6

Published by Arcadia Publishing,
an imprint of the Chalford Publishing Corporation,
One Washington Center, Dover, New Hampshire 03820.
Printed in Great Britain

Library of Congress Cataloging-in-Publication Data applied for

OTHER PUBLICATIONS BY WALTER K. SCHRODER:

Defenses of Narragansett Bay in World War II

Stars and Swastikas: The Boy Who Wore 2 Uniforms

Contents

This detail from a 1777 chart of the Bay of Narragansett by Charles Blaskowitz shows the strategic location of Dutch Island in the West Passage of the bay, as well as nearby ferry landings which were vital to the island garrison. (University of Rhode Island Special Collections.)

Introduction

Dutch Island is one of a number of islands located within the confines of Narragansett Bay, Rhode Island. Motorists crossing the West Passage of the bay via the Jamestown Bridge will notice the 81-acre island to the south, situated in the center of the channel, midway between Jamestown (Conanicut Island) and Saunderstown on the mainland. Although some commuters make the crossing frequently, few pay much attention to that peaceful spot of land well within their view. Even fewer know the name of the island, or realize that the remains of a few distinguishable structures and the high green mounds that are clearly visible are evidence of an abandoned coastal defense site known as Fort Greble, and an 80-year military presence that saw its beginnings during the Civil War period. Today, Fort Greble is no more and Dutch Island is included in Rhode Island's Island Parks System, one of several sites in Narragansett Bay designated as recreational areas for the benefit of the public.

It is difficult to appreciate the many fascinating changes that took place in the course of the island's development, some in rapid succession. A brief look at the more significant historical benchmarks may provide a better understanding of this evolution.

Known as Quetenis Island, the site was sold to the Dutch West India Company by the Narragansett Indians in 1636–37. They used the area as a trading post for approximately twenty years and are said to have fortified the island during that time, but there is no physical evidence to support this theory. English settlers from Newport later acquired rights to use the island as pasturage for their sheep. In 1825, the United States Lighthouse Service acquired approximately 6 acres of land at the southern tip of the island, and a lighthouse was soon built on the site. This facility was demolished some years later because of poor construction, and a new lighthouse was built in 1857.

The island continued to be used as a pasturage for sheep until 1852, when Powell H. Carpenter purchased the land. In 1864, as the Civil War approached, Carpenter sold the island to the federal government, six months after the governor of Rhode Island, under mandate from the federal government, had ordered the 14th Rhode Island Heavy Artillery Regiment (Colored) to construct defensive earthworks on the island. This was the first time a military garrison had been established on Dutch Island. "Camp Bailey" is the name given to this encampment. The troops are said to have been housed in poorly constructed barracks on the northern end of the island where they suffered severely from cold and smallpox during the winter months. Altogether, sixteen died and were buried in a small cemetery established for them on the island.

Two defensive systems were constructed at that time, a temporary earthwork at the central-southeast section of the island, and the so-called "Lower Battery," on the southern tip of the Lighthouse Reservation. When completed, seven 8-inch Columbiads and one 32-pounder were mounted on the temporary earthwork; no guns were installed at the Lower Battery due to its extremely low siting and susceptibility to occasional flooding, which prompted references to that site as the "Wash Tub Battery."

After the Civil War, several new gun batteries were constructed. In 1867, work on a "Middle Battery," designed to mount six 15-inch Rodman guns, was commenced to replace the earlier temporary earthworks. This was completed in April 1869. Construction of a main barbette battery for forty 15-inch guns on the summit of the island was approved in 1870, but the project was never completed. Appropriations were exhausted in 1875 and no further work was done. This was followed by a period of virtual inactivity from 1875 to 1898, after which a new and more ambitious round of coastal defense construction got underway. At that time, the "post on Dutch Island," as it had been known until then, was formally redesignated as Fort Greble.

In 1897, construction of a battery of 10-inch disappearing guns designated as Battery Hale was commenced at the site of the discontinued main barbette battery. This construction was completed a year later. In May 1898, a single emplacement for a 6-inch Quick Firing Gun was built northwest of Battery Hale. In 1903, this position was rebuilt into a battery of three 6-inch rifles mounted on disappearing carriages and named Battery Mitchell. Construction of a mortar battery, later named Battery Sedgwick, got underway on the north side of the island in 1898. This project was completed in 1901 and eight 12-inch mortars were initially mounted (the number was subsequently reduced to four). Finally, in 1900, a battery of two 3-inch 15-pound rapid fire guns, known as Battery Ogden, was built upon the center section of the earlier Middle Battery.

Concurrent with the revitalization and expansion of the gun batteries, an entire military enclave and community, complete in all respects, was created, allowing the post on the island to become a largely self-sufficient entity. Among the various facilities and recreational amenities provided at this fort were post office and post exchange facilities, a bowling alley, bakery, and a tennis court. A hospital was also operational for on-site troop care. Unfortunately, vital supplies needed to be replenished from across the bay and there was a lack of adequate on-site water, which made the naturally protected installation vulnerable to prolonged isolation.

Besides a permanent Coast Artillery cadre, Fort Greble recorded housing as many as 495 transients in available barracks spaces and temporary tent encampments that were erected as needs arose. Most of the men at the fort were from Coast Artillery units of the Rhode Island Militia and National Guard, including some personnel from out of state who also spent time on the island during designated training periods. From time to time the garrison was joined by smaller infantry and cavalry details. Fort Greble was a very active military post during the pre-World War I period, throughout that war, and well into the mid-1920s. Several other coastal defense facilities constructed nearby proved sufficient to the defense of the bay in World War II, rendering Fort Greble a passive partner within the overall Narragansett Bay Harbor Defense System. The Dutch Island facility was generally inactive during World War II, except for its occasional use as a rifle range, and was finally discontinued in 1947.

While the permanent quarters of the officers and noncoms and their families, and the enlisted men's barracks, are now gone, the island still abounds with many indelible features pointing to a significant military presence over a long period of time. The wooden and brick buildings have fallen, but the concrete defensive positions of once powerful long range weapons, modern and highly effective at the turn of the century, remain as silent reminders for generations to see. They are witness to the days when men served their country with pride at duty stations along the coast of Rhode Island. Even the forerunners of the monolithic concrete bastions are still evident in earlier emplacements that had been built of solid blocks of granite, and a trained eye might even detect overgrown earthworks and trenches dating to the days of the Civil War. When active, Fort Greble on Dutch Island was a site of much activity; of troops coming and going for years on end. Now there is silence. Today, Fort Greble remains an important repository of more than eighty years of Rhode Island military history; it is a virtual open air museum waiting to be acknowledged and appreciated.

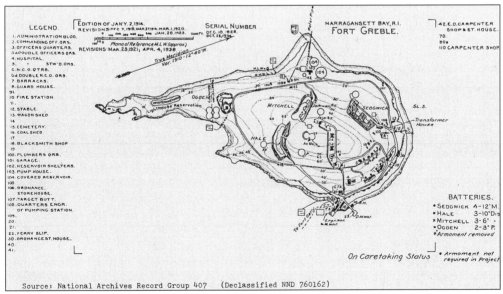

This map of Fort Greble, last updated in 1938, provides an overview of the various facilities and gun batteries located on Dutch Island at that time. The marginal legends identify the sites and buildings as well as the status of the various defensive positions. (National Archives and Records Service.)

On May 31, 1898, the "Post on Dutch Island" was officially designated Fort Greble, in honor of Lieutenant John T. Greble, 2nd Artillery, who was one of the first regular army officers killed in action in the Civil War. He was born in Philadelphia on January 9, 1834, and fell at Big Bethel, Virginia, on June 10, 1861. (Courtesy of Don Harvey.)

One

Civil War and the Post
on Dutch Island

Dutch Island Light was perhaps the first permanent structure built on the island. In 1825, a 6-acre parcel was acquired at the southern tip of the island by the United States Lighthouse Service and the first lighthouse was constructed shortly thereafter. It was rebuilt in 1857 and appeared as shown here. (Author's Collection.)

In 1878, a machine-operated fog bell was installed at the lighthouse. It functioned like a clock and had to be wound up every few hours. The light station gave off its own unique series of rings and mariners would know their location by the sound and frequency of the bell. (National Park Service.)

Looking north from the lighthouse tower, several buildings erected at Fort Greble between 1900 and 1904 can be seen at the top of the picture, including the fence separating the Lighthouse Reservation from that of the military. The earth mounds at the left are part of the Lower Battery, a Civil War gun emplacement. (Courtesy Sue Maden.)

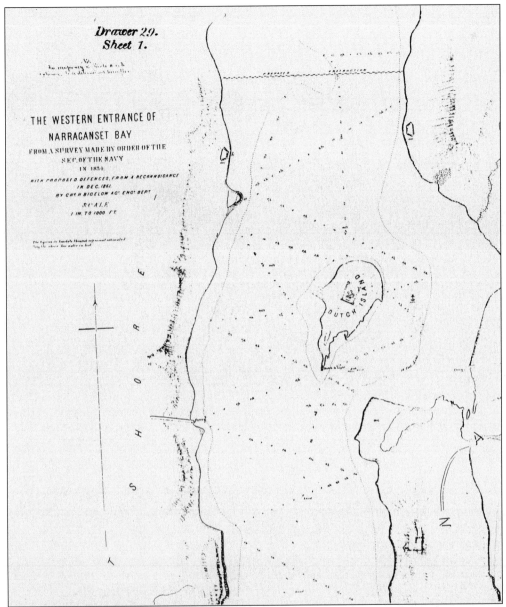

Drawer 29.
Sheet 1.

THE WESTERN ENTRANCE OF
NARRAGANSET BAY

FROM A SURVEY MADE BY ORDER OF THE
SEC. OF THE NAVY
IN 1834.
WITH PROPOSED DEFENCES, FROM A RECONNOISANCE
IN DEC. 1861.
BY CAP.N BIGELOW AC.T ENG.R DEPT

SCALE
1 IN. TO 1000 FT.

DUTCH ISLAND

S H O R E

N

Based on a survey of 1834, a plan was developed in 1861 to close the western entrance of Narragansett Bay by placing obstructions across the entire width of the bay just north of Dutch Island, with defensive earthworks on either side of the passage. This plan never materialized. (National Archives and Records Service.)

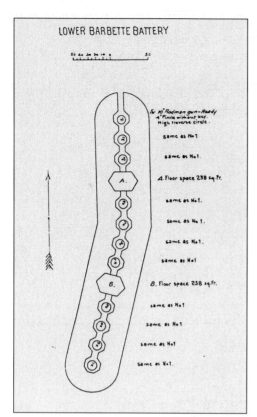

LOWER BARBETTE BATTERY

For 10" Rodman gun - Ready 4" Pintle without key. High traverse circle.

same as No. 1

same as No. 1.

A. Floor space 238 sq. ft.

same as No. 1.

same as No. 1.

same as No. 1.

same as No. 1

B. Floor space 238 sq. ft.

same as No. 1

same as No. 1

same as No. 1

same as No. 1.

In 1863, the federal government commenced construction of a barbette battery for eleven 10-inch center pintel Rodman guns on the grounds of the lighthouse. Although completed, the Lower Battery, as it was called, was never armed as intended because the site was on low ground, making it susceptible to occasional flooding. (National Archives and Records Service.)

The low, octagonal, open gun emplacements of the Lower Battery were made of finely crafted blocks of granite. They are a lasting monument to the hands that built them and appear capable of withstanding the elements for many more years. This photograph was taken while looking south. (National Park Service.)

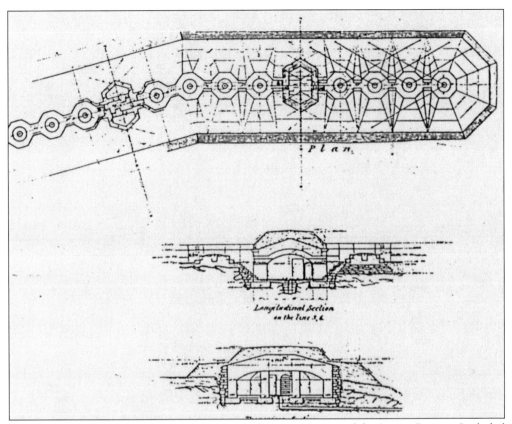

The above plan provides additional details on the construction of the Lower Battery. Included in the alignment of the 11-gun positions are two subterranean magazines, constructed of granite and brick, each measuring 23-by-27 feet. (National Archives and Records Service.)

Each of the magazines of the Lower Battery had two arched doorways to allow for entry from both the north and south. A 5-foot layer of earth was placed on top of the magazines as protection against enemy fire. (National Park Service.)

Rhode Island Governor James Y. Smith was in office during the Civil War. Empowered by the federal government, he ordered the 14th R.I. Heavy Artillery Regiment (Colored) to Dutch Island to construct defensive earthworks. The first units arrived on the island on September 2, 1863, and commenced construction of an eight-gun battery which they completed in early November. (Courtesy Christie Mercurio.)

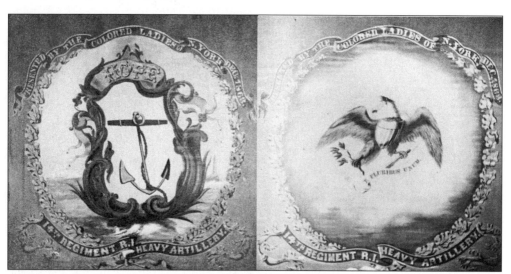

Accompanied by members of the Rhode Island Legislature and other noted guests, Governor Smith visited Dutch Island on November 12, 1863, where he received a fifteen-gun salute on arrival. During a troop review, he presented Rhode Island's 14th "Corps d' Afrique," with a regimental flag closely resembling the above design by Philadelphia artist David B. Bowser. (Photography Collections UMBC.)

16

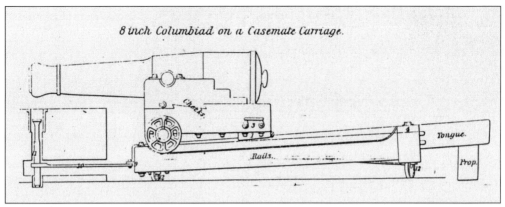

8 inch Columbiad on a Casemate Carriage.

The 14th Regiment entrenched seven 8-inch Columbiads and a 32-pounder in the earthworks they had prepared. The 8-inch guns, mounted on wooden casemate carriages, had been moved to Dutch Island from Fort Warren in Boston. The 32-pounder was shipped in by the New York Arsenal. (Plate 14, *Instructions for Heavy Artillery*, 1862.)

Captain Thomas W. Fry was in charge of Company A, the first unit dispatched to Dutch Island on September 2, 1863. While serving with the U.S. 11th Colored Heavy Artillery in 1864, he dedicated an inscribed Confederate sword to his Excellency Governor Smith. This unique Civil War trophy is now in the museum collection of the Newport Artillery Company. (From *A History of the R.I. Fourteenth Regiment*.)

The original earthworks constructed in 1863 by the 14th Regiment extended from the trench (just below the beach in the upper left) to the lower right side of this aerial photograph. A concrete, 3-inch, two-gun emplacement built in 1900, named Battery Ogden, sits on top of the older Middle Battery, a multi gun position that had been constructed in 1867 upon the right flank of the earlier earthworks. The square structure is a mining casemate, built in 1907. (National Oceanographic and Atmospheric Administration.)

A 70-by-20-foot cemetery was established along the northeast shore of Dutch Island in 1863. It became the burial site for sixteen members of the 14th R.I. Heavy Artillery Regiment (Colored), many of whom had died of smallpox that year. A 7-foot tall obelisk of granite was dedicated in their honor in 1873. The remains of these men were eventually moved from the island in 1948 and reinterred at the Long Island National Cemetery, in Farmingdale, NY, in July of that year. (Jamestown Historical Society.)

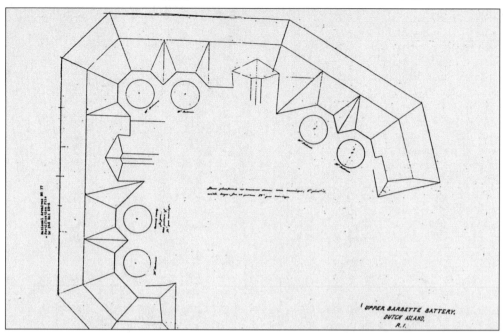

In 1867, the right flank of the temporary 8-gun Civil War earthworks was dismantled and construction of a newer Middle Battery, designed to house six 15-inch Rodman guns, commenced. Completed in 1869, this high earthwork position consisted of chest-high interior walls made of large granite blocks. (National Archives and Records Service.)

In 1869, the Middle Battery consisted of five 15-inch, center pintel, smooth bore, muzzle loading, Rodman guns, each weighing approximately 25 tons. These cannons required a black powder charge of 50 pounds to hurl a 300-pound cannon ball a distance of 3 miles. The gun tubes originated from the Watertown Arsenal. The 15-inch Rodmans on Dutch Island were similar to the guns at Fort Warren in Boston, shown here. The sixth gun position was left vacant. (Courtesy Newport Artillery Company.)

In May of 1870 it was decided to construct a main barbette battery on the summit of the island, capable of mounting forty 15-inch smooth bore guns. Work was curtailed and stopped in 1875, however, due to lack of funds and technological advances in weaponry. The work that had been accomplished was removed to make way for a modern 10-inch gun battery that became known as Battery Hale. The above drawing shows an undated design for a complete fort at that site, which never materialized. (National Archives and Records Service.)

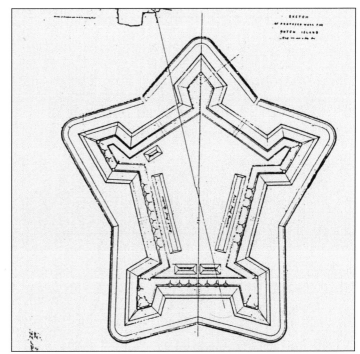

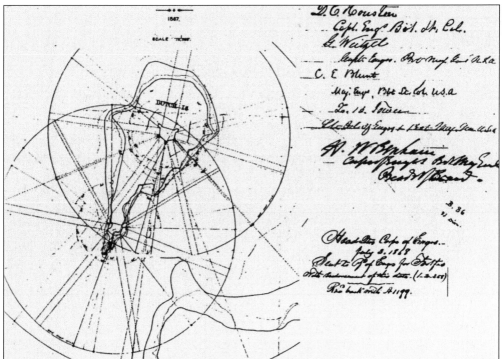

The above plan, dated July 1868, shows the sectors of fire of the Lower Battery, situated on the Lighthouse Reservation at the southern end of Dutch Island, as well as the sectors of fire of the proposed main barbette battery, which was never completed. (National Archives and Records Service.)

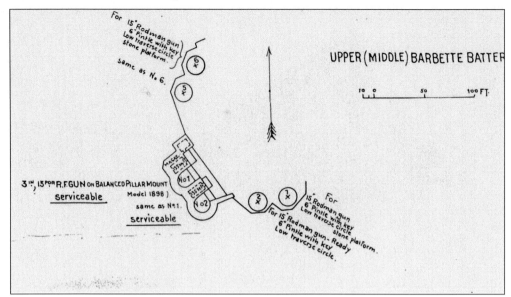

The above sketch shows that 15-inch Rodman gun platforms numbers 3 and 4 of the Middle Battery gave way, in 1900, to the 3-inch rapid fire battery known as Battery Ogden. The Rodman position numbers 1 and 2 were obliterated in 1907 as a result of the construction of a mine casemate at the site of these two guns. (National Archives and Records Service.)

Battery Ogden is shown here in April 1980. The position, completed in April 1900, housed two 3-inch rapid fire guns. Battery Ogden was named in honor of 1st Lt. Frederick C. Ogden, 1st U.S. Cavalry, who was killed at the battle of Trevillian Station, Virginia, on June 11, 1864. (National Archives and Records Service.)

Battery Ogden mounted two 3-inch, 15-pounder rapid fire guns, balanced on pillar mounts, similar to the one shown here. It was the mission of this battery to protect mine fields in the western passage of Narragansett Bay. The location of the guns allowed for "all-around fire," except for sectors that may have been obscured by other island structures. The guns were dismantled in 1921. (Author's Collection.)

A mine commander's station was constructed in 1908, immediately to the rear and left of Battery Ogden. The structure contained two separate stations, each consisting of an observation room, plotting room, and telephone booths. In 1909, a power plant was put into service in an adjacent 22-by-54-foot structure. The above photograph shows both buildings as they appeared in 1980. (National Park Service.)

From the south, the mine commander's station was well protected and camouflaged against enemy observation. The station was constructed so nothing more than the observation slits protruded above the embankment, which provided protection on three sides of the structure against enemy fire. (National Park Service.)

This 1983 photograph shows the mine commander's station after a fire had destroyed the reinforced frame structure that housed the two concrete pedestals upon which delicate optical measuring instruments were once mounted. The tops of the pedestals are 50 feet above the mean low water mark. (Author's Collection.)

Two

Dutch Island becomes Fort Greble

In 1898, three 10-inch breech-loading rifles on disappearing carriages, closely resembling the gun above, were mounted at the summit of Dutch Island, at the site of the earlier planned main barbette battery. A modern emplacement of Rosendale cement with Portland facing, designated as Battery Hale, had been constructed during the preceding year to receive these weapons. The guns were sited 75 feet above the mean low water mark. (Collection of Alfred K. Schroeder.)

Constructed during 1897–98, Battery Hale was named in honor of Captain Nathan Hale of the American Revolutionary Forces. He was captured by the British and hanged as a spy in 1776. This battery comprised positions for three 10-inch guns on disappearing carriages. Each gun was assigned 120 rounds of ammunition that were stored in magazines at the lower level of the emplacement. (National Park Service.)

An elevator located near each of Battery Hale's three guns was utilized to bring shells and gun powder from the lower level magazine areas to the upper level of the emplacement, where the shells were moved onto carts and transported to the guns by assigned crews. The elevator shafts are located under the concrete canopies that can be seen in the above picture. During the early 1900s, Battery Hale was an integral part of a coastal defense system assigned the protection of the western entrance to Narragansett Bay in coordination with the armaments of Fort Getty, in Jamestown, and of Fort Kearny, on the mainland. (National Park Service.)

In this 1980 photograph, the designation of a "powder room" painted at an entrance way to the lower level of Battery Hale is still visible. Army records note that the various areas below the gun positions, including powder and shell rooms, the shell gallery, and the alley ways, were fair in winter, but were very damp in the summer. Overhead trolleys were used to move shells from the magazines to the elevators. (National Park Service.)

The gun crew in this picture has raised the gun's tube so it protrudes above the parapet. This is the normal position for this type of gun to fire. After it has been discharged, the interaction of the recoil with the hydraulic mechanism of the disappearing carriage lowers the tube and locks it in a position behind and to the rear of the parapet, where it can then be reloaded, shielded from the danger of enemy observation. The guns and carriages of Battery Hale were dismounted in 1943. (Courtesy Thomas J. Peirce.)

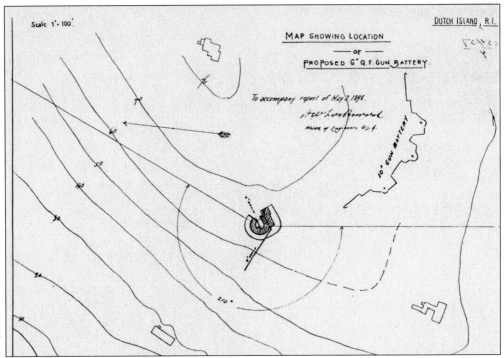

MAP SHOWING LOCATION
— OF —
PROPOSED 6" Q.F. GUN BATTERY.

DUTCH ISLAND, R.I.

To accompany report of May 2, 1898.

Construction of an emplacement and magazine for a single 6-inch quick fire, pedestal mounted, Armstrong gun, just west of Battery Hale, was commenced in May 1898 and the gun was mounted in August of that year. In 1899, the Coast Artillery took charge of this site and the responsibility of covering the channel north of the island and the minefield in that area. (National Archives and Records Service.)

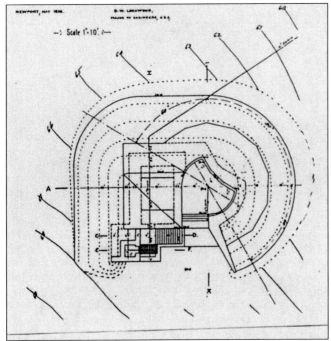

In 1903, the single gun position, shown here in greater detail, was taken over by the Army Engineers for the purpose of rebuilding and expanding the site into a battery of three 6-inch guns, mounted on disappearing carriages. The upgraded position became known as Battery Mitchell. (National Archives and Records Service.)

The construction and installation at Battery Mitchell of three 6-inch breech loading rifles, mounted on disappearing carriages, was completed in January 1906. The gun shown here is behind the parapet in a lowered position where it is protected from enemy observation. When ordered, the crew would raise the tube above the parapet and send a projectile in the direction of the chosen target. This photograph is of a similar type gun installed at Fort H.G. Wright. (Collection of Alfred K. Schroeder.)

Taken in 1912, this photograph shows a Fort Greble gun crew loading one of the 6-inch disappearing guns of Battery Mitchell. Presently, the shell is being rammed into the gun tube. It would be followed by the powder charge which has been lifted from the transport cart by one of the crew members. The gun is in the lowered position and protected by the parapet during the loading operation. (Collection of Alfred K. Schroeder.)

Battery Mitchell was named in honor of Captain David B. Mitchell, 15th U.S. Infantry, who was killed on September 17, 1900, in action with insurgents near Luzon, in the Philippine Islands. The naming of this, and other sea coast forts and batteries, was as directed by the President, and implemented by the secretary of war. The above picture shows two of the three gun platforms with the view to the south. (National Park Service.)

Several anti aircraft guns were installed on the parapet of Battery Mitchell. This is one of the platforms as it appeared in 1980. (National Park Service.)

The magazines that occupied the lower level of Battery Mitchell were termed "dry and excellent at all times." Each of the three magazines had a storage capability for 205 rounds of ammunition (shells and powder charges). Some of the storage areas were lined with a layer of glazed bricks. (National Park Service.)

While the guns and carriages of Battery Mitchell were removed and dismounted by 1921, the lower level storage and magazine areas continued to be utilized for some time. The Battery Mitchell power plant was utilized to supply the power for Battery Hale until the early part of World War II. It is said that the magazine areas were also used to store explosives and underwater mines that were ultimately moved to Jamestown and placed in storage at Fort Wetherill. (National Archives and Records Service.)

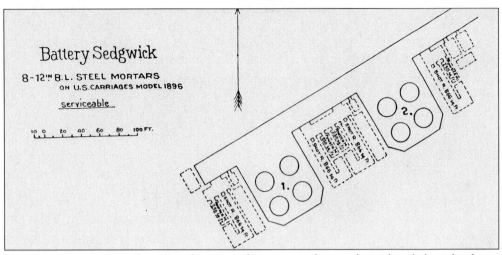

In 1898, construction of a 12-inch mortar battery on the north side of the island was commenced, consisting of two firing pits, each with four mortars. The work was completed two years later. The above sketch shows the general layout of the mortar positions as well as the powder and shot magazines. (National Archives and Records Service.)

Mortars were capable of firing in a high trajectory. Utilized in a coastal defense setting, the aim would be to penetrate the decks of enemy ships, as opposed to hitting the hulls as would the guns of Batteries Hale and Mitchell. This 1912 photograph shows one of the mortars of Battery Sedgwick as it is being fired. Note the steep elevation of the tube. (Collection of Alfred K. Schroeder.)

In this unusual photograph, the shell is just leaving the muzzle of a 12-inch mortar in a steep trajectory, while several of the men are protecting their ears from the sound of the loud explosion. Carts with additional shells are lined up, ready for loading the next round. (Courtesy Sue Maden.)

Four of the eight 12-inch mortars of Battery Sedgwick were removed in 1918 and the vacant gun positions filled in. This action gave the gun crews more space in which to work, which had a positive effect on the rate of fire that could be attained. The removed parts were stored at Fort Greble for close to twenty years. In 1942 the mortars were removed from the island and made available for reutilization. (Courtesy Thomas J. Peirce.)

The mortar battery at Fort Greble was named in honor of Major General John Sedgwick, U.S. Volunteers, who had distinguished himself in the Mexican and Civil Wars. He was killed at the battle of Spottsylvania, on May 9, 1864. At the time of his death he commanded the 6th Corps, Army of the Potomac. This photograph is of the battery commander's position next to and in the line of view of the mortar pits. (Author's Collection.)

The generators for the Fort Greble power plant were housed in a structure of solid concrete near Battery Sedgwick on the north side of the island. The building is described as having 2-foot exterior walls of concrete and a roof 2 to 4 feet thick, covered in places with a 9-foot layer of earth and stone. (National Archives and Records Service.)

34

Battery Sedgwick's power was derived from the generating equipment installed in this structure of concrete. The building was divided into three areas, separated by 1-foot walls, that contained the boiler room, engine room, and accumulator room. While in an active status, the building was reported as being generally dry. (National Archives and Records Service.)

In this picture the thick layer of earth, covered with natural growth, can be readily seen on top of the Battery Sedgwick power plant. Though built in 1901, the structure and chimney have weathered the elements well over the years. (Author's Collection.)

35

Activities in these mortar pits during the days when Fort Greble was an active military installation, can hardly be imagined by anyone who is unfamiliar with the history and the development of Dutch Island. Too strong and solid to be obliterated, these concrete monuments will continue to serve as silent reminders of the military presence on Dutch Island for future generations to see and wonder about. (National Park Service.)

In 1902, a three-story, 15-by-17-foot fire commander's station of red brick and concrete was constructed on high ground northeast of Battery Mitchell. This command structure, sited in close proximity to the senior officers' quarters, was on a site where the height and location allowed for the oversight and control of the three gun installations to the south, i.e. Batteries Mitchell, Hale, and Ogden. Access to the command spaces was via a narrow exterior stairway. (National Park Service.)

A second fire commander's station was constructed to the rear of Battery Hale. This structure was also of brick and concrete, but was smaller than the original 3-story command facility, which was located a short distance away. The building was of sufficient height to afford the observers assigned to the optical instruments an open view to the waters south of the island. The exterior appearance of the structure appears good in this 1983 photo. (Author's Collection.)

Vandals inflicted considerable damage on the smaller of the two fire commander's stations as can be seen from this photo taken in 1996. A large section of brickwork has been removed from around the observation slit, and much of the heavy colored glass that had been installed in the ceiling for the deflection of light is now gone. (Author's Collection.)

A mining casemate was constructed on the northern shore of Dutch Island in 1898. The *Newport Journal*, dated March 5 of that year, described it in part as "an underground cell, deep down in Mother Earth, to which entrance is secured by winding passages, so that the occupants and apparatus are perfectly secure from danger from the most severe bombardment from without." (National Park Service.)

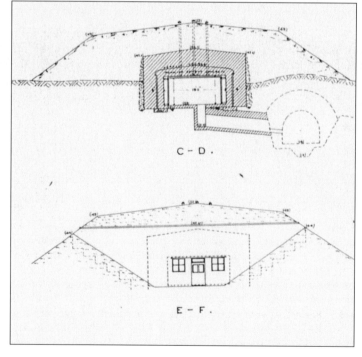

This 1899 drawing of the mining casemate does not reveal any winding passages, as described above. The *Newport Journal* of March 5, 1898, went on to say that "from these chambers there leads a cable tunnel, emerging below the low water mark. In the navigable channels round about there are planted powerful submarine mines, and these are connected with the casement leading in through the cable tunnel." The latter information appears accurate. (National Archives and Records Service.)

Three

The Military Community—A Look at the Facilities

Construction of the permanent housing and supporting facilities necessary to maintain a military post and garrison on Dutch Island commenced in 1898, and continued for about five years. An array of diversified structures comprising the Fort Greble military community can be seen in this photo taken in the 1930s from aboard an approaching ferry. The Engineer's Wharf is to the left and the Quartermaster's Wharf to the right. Both docks had adequate space and facilities. The building on the hill between the two docks is the hospital, and to the right of it are two of the 109-man barracks. The buildings in the rear include officers quarters and housing for enlisted staff members. (Photo by Harold Sherman.)

The double officers quarters were quite appealing to the eye. Two identical structures were erected at Fort Greble in May 1900, providing quarters for the families of four lieutenants. The frame buildings were built on stone and brick foundations and had a total floor area above their basements of 2,904 square feet. Overall construction cost was $10,272 per building. These houses were provided with electricity, water, steam heat, and plumbing. (National Archives and Records Service.)

This photograph, taken in 1980, shows the remains of the double officers quarters at that time. The buildings, along with many others on Dutch Island, were turned over to the National Youth Administration in November 1938 and dismantled. Construction records show that the island's sanitary and storm drains were combined and the sewage discharged into the bay. (National Park Service.)

A total of four single officers quarters were constructed between 1901 and 1902. Two of these buildings were identical in size and appearance. Two others were somewhat larger and were modified with individualized construction features. One field grade officer and three captains and their families occupied these family homes, which ranged in cost from $7,465 to $11,013. In these buildings, the floor space above the basement ranged from 2,373 to 3,265 square feet. (National Archives and Records Service.)

A survey of the island conducted by the National Park Service in April 1980 documented the condition of one of the single officers quarters as shown above. This building had also been turned over to the National Youth Administration forty-two years earlier. Waste disposal during the days when Fort Greble was active, was by burial, burning, or other methods. (National Park Service.)

The homes of the officers and their families were built side-by-side along a macadam road leading in a westerly direction uphill from the dock area. This section was called "Officer's Row." The colors displayed from a nearby 75-foot metal flagstaff could be readily seen from the mainland and Jamestown. A tennis court was laid out in front of the family houses. (Courtesy Joeseph E. Coduri.)

One has difficulty associating this deteriorating and cracking slab of concrete deep within a patch of briar with the tennis court that provided a means for relaxation to the island's military tenants, little more than half a century ago. The tennis court was located near the flagstaff on the northern edge of an open area that was used as a drill field and parade ground. (Author's Collection.)

This view shows the 75-foot metal flagstaff with the guy wires and shackles that were needed to securely anchor the pole at the crest of the island, where strong winds prevail in stormy weather. One of the fort's saluting guns near the flagstaff was fired every morning at the flag raising, and again at sundown when the flag was lowered and retired for the night. (National Archives and Records Service.)

In this 1996 photograph, the abandoned flagstaff had given way to the elements and time, collapsing where it once had proudly flown the Stars and Stripes high above the island. Only the concrete foundation that was poured in 1903 and the pole's mounting fixture remain intact as silent reminders of the island communities' days of glory. (Author's Collection.)

43

All in all, there were four double non-commissioned officer's quarters on the island. These had been built at different times (1900, 1903, and 1909) to provide family housing for noncoms of the permanent cadre. The houses were laid out beside a road to the rear of a number of larger troop barracks that were built near the shore. Construction costs ranged from $3,193 to $7,102 for the buildings, two of which were heated by hot air. The other two were heated by stoves. All units were comparable in size, with available floor space above the basements ranging from 1,576 to 1,650 square feet. (National Archives and Records Service.)

The double NCO quarters were also donated to the National Youth Administration in 1938, leaving little to the elements. In this 1980 photograph, only portions of brick wall sections and the foundation remain. All of the buildings had slate roofs originally. (National Park Service.)

Three large troop barracks were constructed along the eastern side of the island. The first structure (left) is a wooden frame building, built in 1900, with a capacity for housing 100 men in 6,009 square feet of floor area. The second wooden barracks, completed in 1901, had 9,677 square feet of floor space, housing an additional 100 men. In 1918, the porches of both buildings were enclosed to provide billeting space for up to 50 additional personnel per building. The barracks at the right is a brick structure built in 1910 with billeting spaces for 109 men. (Courtesy Joeseph E. Coduri.)

Nothing more than the stone foundations and some debris was left of the wooden barracks when this photo was taken in 1980. In 1900 and 1901, the construction costs for the two wooden barracks buildings had amounted to $30,883 and $28,826, respectively. Each of the buildings was outfitted with 109 wall lockers. Congress created the Artillery Corps at the time of construction, setting the strength of Coast Artillery companies at 109 men. These buildings were among those turned over to the National Youth Administration in 1938. (National Park Service.)

In 1910, this brick barracks set upon a brick foundation was constructed at a cost of $41,613. The 12,329-square-foot building was heated by steam and had a capacity of housing 109 troops. Overall measurements of the building were 142-by-46 feet, with a 37-by-38-foot wing off the rear center section. (National Archives and Records Service.)

A fire destroyed the interiors and roof of the brick barracks sometime in the 1970s, long after Fort Greble had been disbanded. The arched, red brick structure on the east side of Dutch Island had long been a special landmark to many people across the water in Jamestown. Observers were saddened to see the only habitable structure remaining on the island go up in flames. (Author's Collection.)

The exterior walls of this one-time gem in barracks styling stand as silent guardians on the eastern shore of Dutch Island, outward reminders of the Army's presence at this isolated island post in years past. Although often erroneously referred to as "The Hospital," the impressive 1910 brick barracks building, despite its present condition, commands the attention and respect of many, a sign that Fort Greble is more than memory. (Author's Collection.)

This is the interior front porch area of the fire-gutted enlisted barracks as it appeared in 1980. It is evident that the brickwork had been executed with perfect workmanship when built. One might contemplate who the soldiers may have been that walked these halls at an earlier time, and wonder whether they returned from the Great War after being shipped overseas from here during World War I. (National Park Service.)

The docks were located on the eastern side of Dutch Island. The 240-foot-long Quartermaster's Wharf (at the left) was constructed of piles and planking and had a 40-by-47-foot wing. This dock was destroyed by the 1938 hurricane. On the right is the Engineer's Wharf. It was faced with large granite stones and then backfilled. A coal shed and a building containing a cable tank were at the wharf site. A 12-foot-wide macadam road system, combined with concrete and gravel walkways, made all essential areas on the island readily accessible. (Courtesy Sue Maden.)

In this winter scene, ice-floes can be seen in the water off Fort Greble and in Dutch Harbor, near the East Ferry area of Jamestown. The Quartermaster's Dock at the fort is deserted as landing was difficult, if not impossible, whenever ice had formed on the bay. The structures at the dock are boat houses for five row boats and a barge. (Courtesy Joe Bains.)

48

Coal was an important commodity to the island community, especially during winter months when living quarters required heating fuel in addition to the normal daily consumption needed to keep the fort operating. This frame and corrugated iron coal shed, capable of storing 700 tons of coal, was built at the Engineer's Wharf in 1900. The building was 21-feet wide by 111-feet long and had four storage bins comprising 2,258 square feet of the available floor area. The structure had a corrugated iron roof, but no lights or heat. (National Archives and Records Service.)

This is the Engineer's Wharf as it appeared in 1980. Only the foundations of the earlier structures remain. Tracks needed to move carts to the coal shed and storage buildings during unloading operations are embedded underfoot. (National Park Service.)

In 1899 this building was constructed and used as a temporary officers quarters. It was moved and converted into offices in 1900, when it became the island's administration building. (Courtesy Joeseph E. Coduri.)

This is a 1900 view of the administration building after it had been moved and reconstituted into office spaces. The 25-by-48-foot structure was ultimately sited on the slope above and near the hospital, where "Officer's Row" began. The building had steam heat and a slate roof. The post office of Fort Greble operated from these spaces for twelve years that included the World War I period. (National Archives and Records Service.)

Along with other construction in 1900, a 1,513-square-foot guard house was erected that could accommodate a guard squad and thirteen prisoners. The 34-by-53-foot frame building sat on a brick foundation, had a slate roof, and was heated by steam. Cost of construction is recorded as $4,591. The guard house was located opposite the docks, and was the first building new arrivals would see after leaving the wharf area. (National Archives and Records Service.)

The post exchange was completed in 1901 at a cost of $13,935. It was a 44-by-94-foot building that had an 18-by-26-foot wing, frame walls, a roof of slate, and a foundation of stone and brick. The structure was heated by a hot water system. Recreational facilities within the building included a 36-by-44-foot gymnasium on the first floor and a billiards and reading room. A 14-by-89-foot bowling alley was in the basement. Regretfully, the building was totally destroyed by fire in February 1920. (National Archives and Records Service.)

Fort Greble had a twelve-bed post hospital, built in 1904 at a cost of $22,872, which was constructed in accordance with plans and specifications of the Surgeon General. The building was T-shaped with a 42-by-44-foot main section and a 25-by-44-foot wing. As with most buildings at the fort, the hospital was of frame construction with a stone foundation and slate roof. Heating was by hot water. There were three floors above ground, with the floor area totalling 5,532 square feet. (National Archives and Records Service.)

A bakery was constructed in 1900, at a cost of $3,033. The 22-by-44-foot frame structure had a brick foundation and slate roof, and could provide 280 rations daily, sufficient for a two-company post. There are accounts that recall the sweet aroma of freshly baked bread being detected on Jamestown when the wind was blowing in the right direction. (National Archives and Records Service.)

In 1899, a 7,463-square-foot building laid out in the shape of a horseshoe was constructed on the high ground along the shore just south of the docking area. Initially used as a temporary barracks for troops, it was later converted into the quartermaster's commissary storehouse. The main building was 20-by-117 feet and the two wings were 20 feet wide and 153 feet and 134 feet long, respectively. On November 1, 1932, the east wing and portions of the north wing were severely damaged by high winds. As a result, parts of the building had to be demolished. (National Archives and Records Service.)

In 1902, a 24-by-28-foot frame building with a slate roof was built on a stone and concrete foundation on a bluff above the western shore of the island, not far from the reservoir area. This two-story, one-family structure became known as the pump station engineer's quarters. The building, which had an area of 887 square feet, was heated by stoves. Total construction costs amounted to $3,500. (National Archives and Records Service.)

A 1,867-square-foot stable, capable of housing two horses, was built on the northern end of the island near the mortar battery, and in close proximity to other quartermaster facilities. The wood frame structure was constructed at a cost of $4,597. In 1902, a double stall was added and interior partitions changed. The building was not heated. (National Archives and Records Service.)

There existed several ordnance storehouses at the fort over the years. The oldest was built before 1900. It was destroyed by fire in 1923. A second wood framed ordnance facility was erected in 1903, followed by the above building of concrete which was built in 1915. The latter served as a militia storehouse and later for the stocking of ordnance items. It is located near the entrance to the Battery Sedgwick area. This photograph was taken during a 1980 survey. (National Park Service.)

This photograph shows a concrete searchlight shelter that was built into a slope on the west side of Dutch Island. The date of construction is uncertain, but it is estimated to have been before World War I, perhaps as early as 1900. The opening of the two-story structure faced west. From it, a small rail track, mounting a movable tower with a 60-inch searchlight, led to the edge of the water near the reservoirs. This light was used to illuminate the bay and the minefields at night. To this day the exterior of the building shows signs of earlier camouflage markings. (Author's Collection.)

A number of cable huts are located along the shore of the island, through which incoming underwater communication and power cables were tied into the island's system. In 1898, the Providence Telephone Company provided long distance telephone service, via double conductor cable from Fox Hill on Conanicut Island, to the Dutch Island facility. This enabled direct voice communications with superior headquarters at Fort Adams in Newport. Outside electricity was provided as needed by the South County Electric Company, utilizing submerged cables. (Author's Collection.)

In this view from the northeast, an ordnance storehouse can be seen at the left, giving the appearance of standing in front of the brick barracks building. The ordnance storehouse made of concrete is at the far right. To the left of this structure is the mining casemate, and beyond, on the hill, the family homes of the officers and noncoms can be seen. (Photo by Harold Sherman.)

This aerial photograph, taken in 1972, provides a complete overview of Dutch Island and the remains of Fort Greble. The docking area is visible at the far left. Following down the shore line, the outside walls of the large brick barracks can be observed, and to the right the mining casemate and ordnance storage building can be seen. Just above these is Battery Sedgwick. At the far right are the reservoirs, and to their left are Batteries Mitchell and Hale. A close look at the area below these latter two gun emplacements reveals a number of cellar holes situated in a perfect semi circle, where homes once stood. At the upper end of the photograph, Battery Ogden and the mine commander's position are partially hidden by dense growth. Beyond, on the narrow Lighthouse Reservation, is the site of the granite Civil War battery. Dutch Island Light cannot be seen. (L.H.B. Photo.)

It was exciting to approach Fort Greble by boat from Jamestown, as can be seen from this picture taken at a time when all the buildings were in place. In the foreground is the Engineer's Wharf, with several of the industrial structures under the control of the post engineer. These included the coal shed, a cable storage facility, and several warehouse buildings. The dock at the right is the Quartermaster's Wharf, where troops disembarked on arrival by ferry. The buildings in this area included a boat house. Just above this dock are the 109-man wooden barracks. Behind the Engineer's Wharf, the hospital can be seen, and to the left of it is the post exchange facility, also referred to as the YMCA. Still further left is the administration building. (Photo in Author's Collection.)

Four

The Garrison—A Place away from Home

Reveille at the beginning of the day and retreat at sundown have for ages been part of American military tradition. The lowering of the flag at Fort Greble on July 24, 1921, was combined with a parade that followed the retreat ceremony, to which the families and children of garrison members and guests had been invited. Military and civilian dignitaries are seated to the left from where they will review the parading troops. (Jamestown Historical Society.)

Major David Price, commanding officer of Fort Greble during the period from 1905 to 1906, poses with his family on the porch of his quarters. Sitting in the center is Mrs Price; to the left is her mother, Mrs. Peter Hargous. To the right is the daughter of Major Price, Aline Price, who later became Mrs. William Leys of Newport. Fort Greble had a permanent contingent of 201 Coast Artillery personnel assigned during Major Price's tour of duty, consisting of the 72nd and 109th Coast Artillery Companies. (Collection of William Leys.)

Major Price, commanding officer of Fort Greble, poses with his family in front of the C.O.'s home on "Officer's Row" sometime during 1905 or 1906. The family resided in one of the single officers quarters that had been constructed in 1901. (Collection of William Leys.)

Wearing white gloves, the Fort Greble Guard Detachment is being inspected in an area to the rear of the hospital building. A 6-man detail of performing buglers adds to the formality of the occasion. The guard house would be off the picture to the right. Based on the construction date of the hospital and the size of the trees, it is estimated the picture may have been taken in 1905. (Courtesy Joeseph E. Coduri.)

A contingent of National Guardsmen march to the jumpoff point from where they will "Pass in Review" before senior officers on the parade ground located midway between the gun batteries and the officers quarters. In this heavily retouched photograph the detail is carrying the Rhode Island flag besides the national colors. (Jamestown Historical Society.)

In this 1900 photograph, William R. Dillman of the 109th Coast Artillery Company poses while wearing his great coat, cape, and fur skin mittens. The 109th was one of the units recorded as being present at Fort Greble most of the time during the period 1900 to 1915. (Courtesy Karl Dillman.)

James S. O'Brien of the 14th Mine Company can be seen in the center of the top row of this photograph, taken at Fort Greble sometime from 1908 to 1911. Records show frequent movement of this unit during that time. It is said that O'Brien swam from West Ferry in Jamestown to Dutch Island one day, after missing the last ferry back to his post. (Courtesy Kay O'Brien.)

During the summer of 1913, two contingents of the R.I. National Guard, with a strength of about 350 to 380 men each, spent several weeks in training at Fort Greble. Due to the large number of troops on the island, it became necessary for some of the transients to resort to pitching tents. The permanent cadre at that time totalled approximately 284 personnel. (Courtesy Joeseph E. Coduri.)

This photo shows members of the permanent garrison in formation during the summer of 1912. At that time the post housed the 14th, 109th and 110th Coast Artillery Companies, totalling 325 men and 9 officers. They were augmented by 413 R.I. National Guardsmen during the period from July 14 to July 21, and thereafter by 495 troops that arrived on July 21 and left on the July 28. Following the departure of the National Guard, the 109th and 110th Companies

left for Fort Terry, New York, for camp and target practice. These troops shipped out aboard quartermaster steamers *Ayres* and *Branan*. The tall fire commander's station can be seen above left in the photograph, as can several of the officer's family quarters. The saluting gun and caisson are positioned near the flagstaff. (U.S. Army Military History Institute.)

TO THE MEMORY OF

Corporal William W. Lee

From the 109th Company, Fort Greble, R. I.

Killed   AGED

Apr. 2, 1912   31y., 32d.

Beautiful toiler, thy work all done,
Beautiful soul into glory gone,
Beautiful life with its crown now won,
God giveth thee rest.
Beautiful spirit, free from all stain,
Ours the heartache, sorrow and pain,
Thine is the glory, the infinite gain.

The firing of the reveille gun at Fort Greble on April 2, 1912, resulted in the death of Corporal William E. Lee, a member of the 109th Coast Artillery Company. Because of the carelessness of another, a two-pound charge of the wrong gun powder had been loaded which caused the breech block to blow out when Lee pulled the lanyard to discharge the ceremonial gun to awaken the troops that morning. Parts of the steel breech block struck Lee's right lower jaw and entered his brain. He was also hit in the right shoulder and fell to the ground next to the gun. He was given immediate assistance, but his wounds proved to be fatal. (Courtesy Violet (Lee) Doty.)

Corporal Lee (left in front row) and some of his buddies posed in front of their round tent before his untimely death. At that time, 337 permanent personnel were assigned to the fort. Additional transients were also on site for training, which explains the need for the use of tents. Note the field cot inside the tent. Several years before, members of the militia had complained about having to sleep on straw while regular garrison personnel were issued cots. (Courtesy Violet (Lee) Doty.)

Corporal William W. Lee is buried in the Jamestown cemetery known as the "Artillery Lot," across the street from his church. Two hundred and thirty five of his comrades from Fort Greble participated in his funeral procession, representing the 109th, 110th, and 14th Coast Artillery units then stationed on Dutch Island. The 7th Coast Artillery band from Fort Adams was also present. (Author's Collection.)

Dutch Island had been a quiet place from 1875 to 1885, when only thirteen people inhabited the island. It was even quieter in 1889, when the island was garrisoned by no more than a lone ordnance sergeant and his family. That situation changed considerably after the new batteries and supporting facilities were constructed. Commencing about 1898, troops began arriving frequently by the boat load, as this picture shows. (Courtesy Sue Maden.)

A new contingent of troops arrives at Fort Greble in 1915. Movement of personnel was via the Quartermaster's Wharf, where transports and ferries tied up for embarkation or debarkation of the troops. The engineer's docking area begins at the coal shed, on the right. (Author's Collection.)

Although Fort Greble had a limited capacity to board horses other than those needed to move wagons within the post area, a small detachment of horse soldiers could nevertheless be accommodated from time to time. Records dating to 1903 show that a troop from the 2nd Cavalry was on the island at that time. This trooper from the R.I. National Guard is landing his horse in 1921. (Jamestown Historical Society.)

This trooper and his mare are among the select few that represented the cavalry on occasion at the Dutch Island coast artillery installation. Boarding space for the horses was extremely scarce, necessitating enlargement of the existing stable capacity. This was accomplished in 1910. In 1915 a harness and saddle room was moved to a site closer to the quartermaster's stable. (Courtesy Thomas J. Peirce.)

Once arrived and settled in at their home away from home, it was time for Coast Artillery men to pose for a snap shot to send to their families. In the pre-World War I days, militia and National Guard units were required to bring their squad tents to their encampments. At a later time, the tents were prepositioned and stored in the militia storehouse on the island, waiting for the troops to arrive and draw them out. (Courtesy Sue Maden.)

No military installation is complete without a band of its own, or one stationed nearby. The military pageantry, the parades, and the splendor of marching in a uniformed column to the cadence of the drums and music of a military band are things in which soldiers take great pride. The bandsmen in turn receive their reward by heading up the marching column, or witnessing the parade from an off-side position which they assume during certain ceremonies. (Courtesy Sue Maden.)

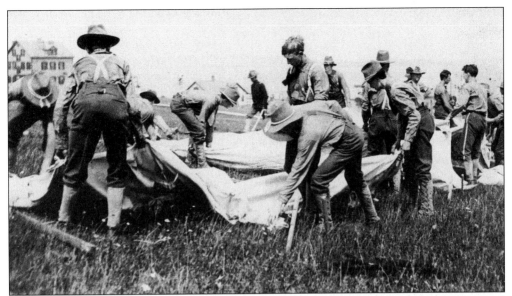

Putting up the large squad tents could be a chore. Here, the 1st Regiment of the R.I. National Guard is hard at work in April 1913. The tents were usually put up on the western side of the island, but this unit appears to be pitching theirs on the parade ground, based on their position in relation to the hospital, which appears in the picture. (Jamestown Historical Society.)

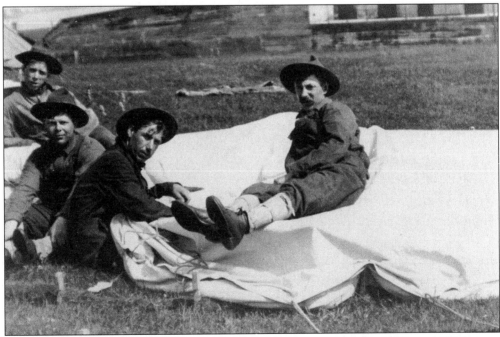

Even the enthusiastic must take a break. Most encampments in the 1920s and 1930s were during the summer months, when woolen uniforms proved unbearable under the rays of the midday sun. Adding physical exertion and perspiration to the formula makes for momentary discouragement, as is evidenced in this picture. (Courtesy Sue Maden.)

This National Guard encampment of wall tents is set up on the west side of Dutch Island, just south of the target butt situated on the waterfront. A boat heading for the South Ferry landing in South Kingstown can be seen near the target area. The trail to the left leads to the reservoirs. (Courtesy Sue Maden.)

Wall tents were preferred by the National Guard. In 1909 the district quartermaster suggested changing from wall tents to the round configuration and storing the tents in a warehouse on the island. Practice had been for the National Guard to move their tents back and forth to Quonset, the state camp ground. (Courtesy Sue Maden.)

During July 1922, members of the 346th Company received a training lecture by their commanding officer, Capt. G.H. Fleck, during their encampment on Dutch Island. Behind them, is the 30-foot-tall fire commander's station, which is accessible only via an outside stairway. The first family home at the upper end of "Officer's Row" can also be seen. (Jamestown Historical Society.)

The Second Battalion of the Second District Coast Artillery Corps, Rhode Island National Guard, passes in review on July 17, 1914. The band is stationed at the right, providing the cadence for the troops on parade. To the rear is the range finder station, and to the right of that is the large quartermaster commissary storehouse, built in 1899. Jamestown can be seen in the distance across the water. (Courtesy Sue Maden.)

Chow time, the time to eat, is a ritual of necessity no one would miss. Mess hall facilities for the transients were set up and operating near the tent area on the western side of the island. The serving line can be seen at the right, perhaps somewhat primitive to civilian likes, but sufficient for hungry troops. A barrel of water containing disinfectant to wash their mess utensils in is set up near the end of the serving line. (Courtesy Joeseph E. Coduri.)

These National Guardsmen find there still is a time for play, despite the daily routine of hard work and training. Humidity and gruelling sun are often present in the Narragansett Bay area during the summer months. Physical activity of choice was a means for the troops to use up excess energy. (Courtesy Joeseph E. Coduri.)

A post office was established at Fort Greble on March 8, 1910, which was operational until May 15, 1922. The first postmaster was John A. Patterson. Before the post office was established at Fort Greble, mail clerks carried the mail to Jamestown. There is a report that one of the men, unable to get a lift, took a rowboat and made the crossing alone. He had a rough passage that took him about an hour, but the mail got through. (Courtesy Sue Maden.)

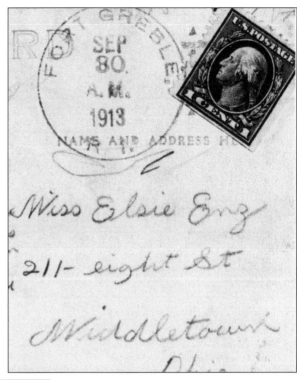

For the entertainment of their loved ones, the men at Greble sent fun messages home when an opportunity presented itself. The YMCA and post exchange were good sources for such postcards and other incidentals, including souvenir kerchiefs and pillow cases. (Courtesy Sue Maden.)

Another group of Rhode Islanders arrives by boat on July 14, 1922. On debarkation, they proceed along the Quartermaster's Dock and head for their camp site across the island, where they will pitch tents and commence training. The men are carrying their individual equipment and assigned rifles, plus any special gear they may need for the duration of their stay. Most Coast Artillery units from the R.I. National Guard spent from one to two weeks on the island each summer. Out of state units would also be detailed to the island on occasion. (Jamestown Historical Society.)

Five

Shortcomings and Logistical Disadvantages

Living on an island can have its drawbacks, especially in winter when the bay may not be navigable because of ice. Such was the case in the winter of 1917, when the ferry *J.A. Saunders* had difficulty approaching the docking facilities. The ice on the bay was sufficiently safe for members of the Fort Greble garrison to meet the ferry off-shore to load and unload. It is noteworthy that the hull of the *J.A. Saunders* was specially designed to permit transporting water to the island. (Irving Sheldon Collection.)

Extreme winter weather conditions in the Narragansett Bay area in 1917 prevented ferries from reaching the dock on occasion. Here, the *J.A. Saunders* drops off passengers so they may walk ashore on the ice, which gives the appearance of being weak in some places. (Irving Sheldon Collection.)

Although there are ice floes on the bay, this ferry was able to approach the Quartermaster's Dock for a regular stop on one of the cold winter days. The ferry does not appear to be under steam, which may account for the inactivity in the docking area. (Courtesy Joe Bains.)

Mishaps do happen. The ferry *J.A. Saunders* went aground along the Dutch Island shore on an undisclosed date. Here, a group of landlubbers is standing by, ready to assist. The low draft allowed the ferry to be refloated at high tide. (Author's Collection.)

The docks were a busy place on Dutch Island. In addition to the departing ferry, a launch and tug boat are tied up at the Quartermaster's Wharf. Several loaded wagons can be observed leaving the dock for their island destinations. To make this somewhat easier there were available approximately 12,000 feet of 12-foot-wide macadam and cinder roads, and some 5,500 feet of walkways that were from 4 to 9 feet wide. (Author's Collection.)

This is one of many ships that frequented the island over the years. The list of visitors includes the sloops *Fashion* and *Argus* in the 1870s, the steamer *Clifford* in 1898, the transports *Kilpatrick* and *General Swartwout* in 1906/7, the ferry *Caswell* in 1902, and the steamer *Squantum* and the mine planters *Major Ringold* and *Gen. Schofield* from 1907 to 1911. Many launches and smaller craft also visited the island, including the *Helena, Agnes, Gretchen,* and *Solicitor,* all of which operated out of Jamestown and Newport. (Courtesy Sue Maden.)

The mine planter *General Richard Arnold* visited Fort Greble repeatedly during the seven-year period preceding World War I. Captained by Peter H. Armbrust of Jamestown until 1916, this mine planter transported and laid mines, carried supplies and personnel to the forts in the bay, towed targets, and during cold winters, broke the ice in the West Passage to assist the ferry traffic. (Courtesy the late Henry Armbrust.)

The *Bay Queen,* an excursion boat operating out of Warren, made stops at Dutch Island in the 1980s, enabling passengers to go ashore by way of a gangplank lowered from the bow. This may have been the first time many visitors ever set foot upon the grounds that once housed Fort Greble, a thriving military installation for close to eighty-five years before it was closed in 1947. In 1958, Dutch Island was declared surplus by the federal government and taken over for conservation purposes by the State of Rhode Island. The State created the Bay Island Park system in 1974 and selected Dutch Island as the first property to be included. (Author's Collection.)

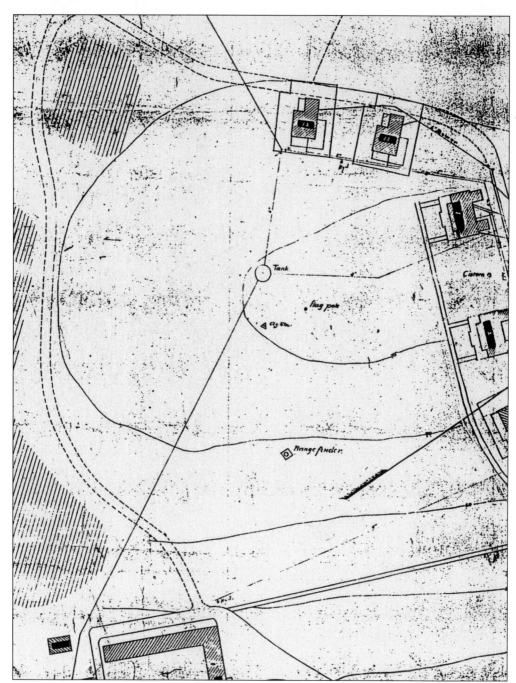

This section of a drawing rendered at some point between 1899 and 1902 shows the single 6-inch gun installation (shaded area) at the top left. The layout of the officer's quarters is apparent, but the two fire commander's positions had not yet been built. Of significance is the water tank near the flag pole. The latter was described in 1889, as "a great water tank of 80 to 90 thousand gallon capacity, which is built in the highest part of the island . . ." This tank, considerable in size, was apparently removed a short time after, as there are no further references to it in later maps or drawings. (National Archives and Records Service.)

Major General Gouverneur K. Warren, Army Engineers, played a significant and continuing role in the military development of Dutch Island. He was instrumental in solving the island's water problem in the early 1870s, when a drilled well and reservoir with a windmill-driven pump were laid on. (Courtesy Don Harvey.)

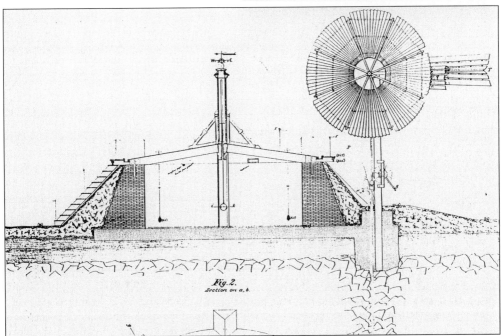

A 120-foot well was drilled in 1873/74 and a round, roof-covered, brick-lined 150,640-gallon distributing reservoir was constructed. During the boring, rubbish specimens were discovered at a depth of 16 feet, 9 inches of the shaft. These were from an older 22.5-foot well that had been drilled in the same place in 1853. (National Archives and Records Service.)

On August 10, 1871, Colonel Thomas Lincoln Casey, visited Dutch Island in the company of Generals G.K. Warren and J.G. Parks. Colonel Casey retired to his farm in Saunderstown that evening, while the generals departed for Newport. Colonel Casey later became chief of Army Engineers. (Courtesy of the Society for the Preservation of New England Antiquities.)

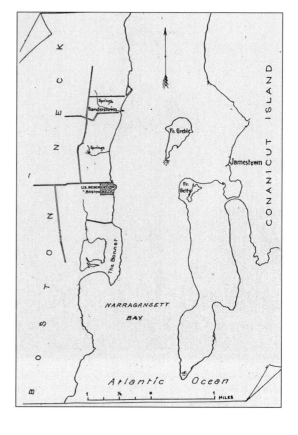

This drawing shows the sites of three springs on the Casey property in Saundertown. The fresh water supply was most advantageous to the garrison on Dutch Island, due to its location on high ground just opposite the island. (National Archives and Records Service.)

The 24.35-acre Saunderstown Reservation containing the springs that supplied Dutch Island was acquired in 1905. The water was gravity fed across the channel through a submarine pipe, pumped into tanks, and distributed to the buildings. Four attempts were made to drive water-producing wells at Fort Greble, all but one without success. The fourth was termed unsafe. (National Archives and Records Service.)

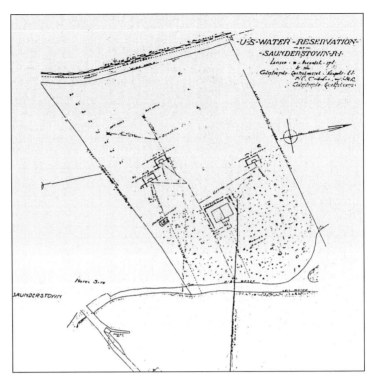

This view shows the 1899 pump house next to a 6,735-gallon water tank located to the rear of the single officer's quarters on "Officer's Row." In 1915, the boiler and pump were dismantled; the building was moved and converted to a harness and saddle room. (National Archives and Records Service.)

This photograph was taken looking from east to west across the island. The reservoir area at the top right includes two underground concrete reservoirs of reinforced concrete that were constructed in 1917, each with a holding capacity in excess of 1 million gallons. Water from the Saunderstown Reservation was fed into these tanks and distributed from there. To the left is a square 71-by-71-foot, 20-foot-deep underground reservoir, built in 1903, that was used to gather rain water. Just below, is the island's first reservoir, built in 1873. This brick-lined structure received a new roof in 1901. Battery Mitchell is in the center of the photograph and Battery Hale is at the left. The tennis court is located between the two brick fire commander's positions. (L.H.B. Photo.)

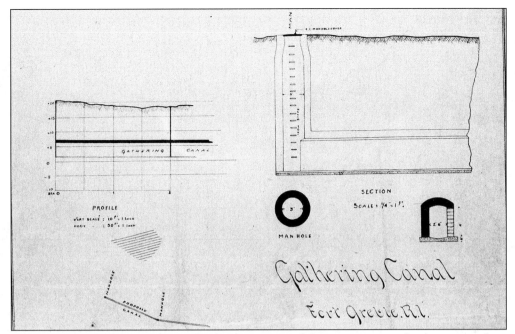

The critical water shortage on Dutch Island necessitated the construction of gathering canals to pick up rain water from the roofs of the houses and feed it into the square reservoir. The canals ran under the west side of the island at a depth of 15 to 20 feet. The canals themselves were 2.5 feet wide and 4 feet high. (National Archives and Records Service.)

The interiors of the 1917 concrete reservoirs give the appearance of modern-day parking garages. Fresh water was gravity fed into the two reservoirs from government-owned springs in Saunderstown. A pump house near the reservoirs maintained the water flow needed to meet the island's needs. (National Archives and Records Service.)

Looking west across the roof of the quartermaster commissary storehouse, the range finder station can be seen in the open field. To the right, next to the last house, the 6,735-gallon steel water tank is clearly visible. Water was pumped into the tank from the reservoir located on flat ground on the west side of the island. (Courtesy Sue Maden.)

For fire protection, a series of fire hydrants were strategically placed around the island. In 1901, a fire station was built and equipped with a hose and ladder truck and two hose carts. Fort Greble was nevertheless dependent on the Jamestown fire station for help in a dire emergency, and in extreme weather conditions, the logistics of moving men and equipment to the island by boat could nullify the impact of any help from the mainland. (National Park Service.)

Six

Neighbors across the Bay

By 1901, the Army had acquired two parcels of land in the West Passage of Narragansett Bay, one at the site of the village of South Ferry, and the other at Fox Hill in Jamestown, upon which it constructed modern-day concrete Coast Artillery fortifications. These sites were named Fort Kearny and Fort Getty, respectively. This event initially placed the responsibility for the protection of the West Passage on the two newer batteries and Fort Greble, which had been the sole defender of the area until that time. Fort Greble remained "on line" and "in the loop" during World War I and well into the 1920s. Thereafter, the geographic location and the logistical shortcomings of the Dutch Island facility could no longer justify its existence. Many of the buildings were dismantled in 1938 and the fort was finally discontinued in 1947. This World War II-era photo shows the active position held by Fort Kearny (left) and Fort Getty (upper right) in blocking the West Passage, with Fort Greble (upper left) in an passive role. (National Archives and Records Service.)

Within view of Dutch Island, Narragansett Village, South Ferry, was situated on the mainland in South Kingstown. Ferries and sloops using the facilities provided the transportation links needed to supply Dutch Island during the Civil War and for years thereafter. This eighteenth-century photograph shows a section of the village at the landing that had been established about 1695. South Ferry Road slopes uphill between the bottom two houses. (Courtesy Thomas J. Peirce.)

South Ferry Church was built in 1850. Sited on high ground, 150 feet above sea level, it has been a landmark for ships plowing the waters of lower Narragansett Bay for over a century. This small church still stands majestically where it was originally built, having outlived most of the other buildings that once comprised Narragansett Village at South Ferry. (Courtesy Thomas J. Peirce.)

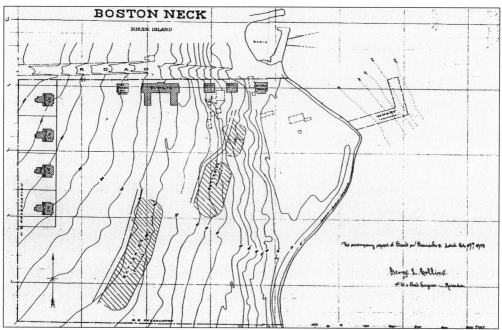

In 1901, the federal government acquired 25 acres of the land at South Ferry, naming it the U.S. Reservation, Boston Neck, where it soon put up military barracks. On December 27, 1904, the site was renamed in honor of Major General Phillip Kearny, U.S. Volunteers. In 1906, several batteries of coastal defense guns were emplaced at this location, just a half mile away from Fort Greble. (National Archives and Records Service.)

One of the old South Ferry buildings was actively used for many years after being taken over by the military. Built in 1845, this 34-by-41-foot stone dwelling was used as a detachment barracks. In 1939, it was designated as quarters for non-commissioned officers, who occupied it during World War II, when Fort Kearny was an active coastal defense facility. The building was razed several years after the war. (National Archives and Records Service.)

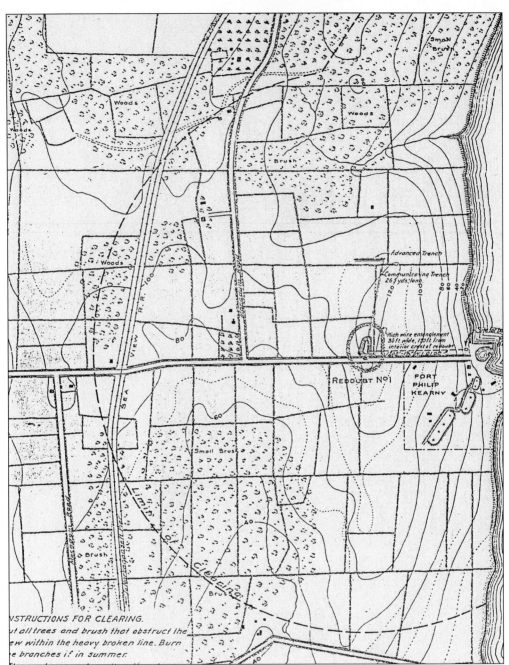

Within the map, the following labels appear:

- Small Brush (upper right)
- Woods (multiple locations)
- Brush
- Advanced Trench
- Communicating Trench 26⅔ yds. long
- High wire entanglement 36 ft. wide, 150 ft. from interior crest of redoubt
- REDOUBT N° 1
- FORT PHILIP KEARNY
- SEA VIEW R.R. 100
- 80
- 60
- 40
- Small Brush
- Limit of Clearing
- Brush
- Narragansett Road

NSTRUCTIONS FOR CLEARING.
t all trees and brush that obstruct the
w within the heavy broken line. Burn
e branches if in summer.

Having constructed a series of coastal fortifications in the Narragansett Bay area that faced the sea, the war department initiated plans in 1912 to provide for the defense of these areas in the event of an attack by land. The plans anticipated the demolition of South Ferry Church and the construction of a redoubt at that site, protected by 36-foot-wide wire entanglements. All stone walls within a 3,000-foot arc of the redoubt were to be knocked down and all trees burned. A similar redoubt was contemplated for nearby Barbers Heights, with additional sites earmarked in Jamestown and Newport. These plans were never implemented, however. (National Archives and Records Service.)

Conanicut Island was linked to Dutch Island and Fort Greble via ferry traffic that generally departed from West Ferry. It was situated on the shortest and most direct route to Fort Adams in Newport, the site of Dutch Island's superior headquarters, and was therefore important to courier traffic and the movement of small military details. This photograph shows West Ferry in the 1880s. (Courtesy Joan Weaver.)

This 1899 photograph shows a steam ferry, the first of its kind to operate between South Ferry in South Kingstown and West Ferry in Jamestown. (Author's Collection.)

Until 1940, passengers and freight were moved to and from Dutch Island and the mainland across the bay, by way of West Ferry. Construction of the Jamestown Bridge in 1940 rendered this service obsolete. This motorized column of the National Guard is waiting for arrival of a ferry, sometime in the 1930s. (Photo Harold Sherman.)

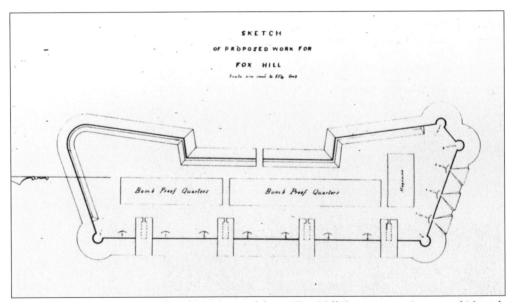

This undated sketch shows a plan for a proposed fort at Fox Hill, Jamestown. A series of 10-inch and 15-inch guns were being considered for installation at this oblong fortification, with the heaviest armament facing south and west. This plan was never implemented. Instead, the government acquired Fox Hill in 1900 and constructed a modern Coast Artillery fortification in the area known as Beaverhead. In May 1903 the site was named in honor of Colonel George W. Getty, 4th U.S. Artillery, Brevet Major General, U.S. Volunteers, who had served with distinction in two wars. (National Archives and Records Service.)

Fort Getty received several gun batteries after the government took over the Fox Hill property. This World War I-era photograph shows one of three 12-inch guns of Battery Tousard, all of which were mounted on disappearing carriages. In addition, two 6-inch pedestal-mounted guns named Battery House, and a smaller emplacement with two pedestal mounted 3-inch guns, were assigned to the concrete positions of this fortified area. (Courtesy Harry Cookson.)

At Fort Getty, a mobile searchlight is set up in 1919, in front of the battery commander's position, located next to 6-inch gun battery House. During World War II the mounted guns were removed from the fort at different times and shipped to other facilities. These actions seemed to foretell the coming demise of Fort Getty. (Courtesy Harry Cookson.)

Postscript

I have written about the military in the Narragansett Bay area before, but finding sufficient materials to warrant a book length discussion of Dutch Island during the last century turned out to be an exceptional challenge. To this day, there are situations that still cannot be adequately documented or verified. These factors account for my many delays in pursuing publication of this historical record until now, more than sixteen years after I first became interested in that silent, almost forgotten place once known as Fort Greble. This book provides not only historical information; it serves as a guide for anyone wishing to explore the island and witness the remains of a military presence that began during the Civil War and ended after the close of World War II. The photographic images and maps have been arranged to provide the reader with an understanding of the developments and happenings on Dutch Island during bygone days, when Rhode Islanders served with pride guarding the entrances to Narragansett Bay.

Acknowledgments

This book incorporates the contributions of many wishing to participate in preserving the memories of Dutch Island and Fort Greble, without whose help this work would not have been possible. I thank each and everyone of them wholeheartedly for their assistance and encouragement during the various phases of the project. In particular, I thank Sue Maden, herself a recognized writer and historian, for unselfishly sharing with me her collection of photographic postcards documenting life at Fort Greble. A special thank you also goes to Joe Bains and Joseph Coduri, both of the What Cheer Postcard Club, for providing copies from their collections. The images and illustrations supplied by the following are very much appreciated: Harry Cookson, Karl Dillmann, Violet Doty, Don Harvey, William Leys, L.H.B. Photo and Alfred Schroeder, Christie Mercurio, Kay O'Brien, Thomas Peirce, Irving Sheldon, Janet Leverone, and Joan Weaver. In addition, I am grateful to the late Henry Armbrust, who provided me with information some years ago. A special word of thanks to the several members of the Council on Americas Military Past, who shared archival data with me over the years.

The following organizations and archives were instrumental in furnishing critical and factual data from the materials at their disposal: the Jamestown Historical Society; the National Archives and Records Service; the National Oceanographic and Atmospheric Administration; the National Park Service, and especially Historian Tom Hoffman; the Newport Artillery Company; the Society for the Preservation of New England Antiquities; the University of Rhode Island Special Collections; the University of Maryland Baltimore County; and the U.S. Army Military History Institute, Carlisle Barracks.

Flow Yoga Sequence: Advanced

SAM SARAHBI

Flow Yoga Sequence: Advanced

ISBN-13: 978-0692656839
ISBN-10: 0692656839